ARELI IS A DREAMER

A TRUE STORY

by **ARELI MORALES,** a DACA recipient

illustrations by **LUISA URIBE**

RANDOM HOUSE STUDIO
NEW YORK

AUTHOR'S NOTE

I was a child of two worlds—a Mexican citizen by birth but raised as an American. The transition to life in America when I was only six was very difficult for me, but the love from my mother, father, and brother made it bearable. Still, living as an undocumented immigrant is scary, and my childhood was filled with secrets and struggles.

My life changed completely when President Barack Obama enacted the Deferred Action for Childhood Arrivals (DACA) program. Through DACA, many Dreamers like me, who came to the United States as children, could remain in the country, have the opportunity to work legally, and even apply for a driver's license. Telling the government about my immigration status was nerve-racking and scary. But after I compiled all the necessary documents, waited anxiously for months, and underwent an intense background check, my application was approved in 2013. I was finally able to come out of the shadows and focus on my dreams. I visited my home country in 2016 and graduated from Brooklyn College in 2018.

Despite the positive outcomes for many young people, the program is constantly being threatened, which places DACA recipients and their families in danger. Although many have tried to terminate the program, the fight for its survival and for permanent and inclusive immigration relief continues. Undocumented immigrants deserve the opportunity to live in this country without fear. I decided to share my story in this book so that young readers could begin to understand what people like me have gone through.

At Abuela's house, Saturdays were filled with family and sunshine. Areli was good at playing *al escondite,* and even better at chasing chickens. She could outrun her big brother, Alex, and their *primas.* When evening came, she sat around a noisy table and ate mounds of tortillas and *pollo con frijoles* for supper—her favorite!

BRIIIIING
BRIIIING

But Sundays were different. On Sundays, Areli and Alex sat in the stuffy living room, waiting and waiting for the phone to ring.

"It's your mamá and papá," said Abuela. "From America!"

"*Hola, Mamá. Hola, Papá,*" said Areli in a small voice.

"*Hola, mi niña,*" said Mamá.

"Did you get the toys we sent you?" asked Papá. Papá always asked about the toys.

"*Si,*" said Areli. "*Gracias, Mamá. Gracias, Papá.*" Mamá and Papá had been away so long, they felt like strangers. "When are you coming home?" she asked. She knew the answer.

"Oh, *mi'ja,* we can't come back to Mexico," said Mamá. "We're trying to get you here to America. With us."

"Your mamá and I dream of the day we will all be together," said Papá. "We will send for you soon. I promise."

When Areli hung up the phone, Alex tried to make her smile. "Mamá and Papá think about us all the time," he said.

"They're working hard, *mi'ja*," Abuela said, "for all of us. They want us to have a better life."

"But why will Alex go to America first, and then me?" Areli asked. Abuela had told her the answer many times.

"Alex was born in America, so he can come and go. You were born here, so it's harder for you."

"How hard?"

Abuela didn't answer. Instead, she wrapped Areli in her arms. "Your mamá and papá want you all to be together. As a family."

But they weren't all together as a family that year. Mamá and Papá didn't come back for Areli's birthday. Or Día de los Muertos. Or even Navidad.

Then one night, Alex took out his suitcase. "Where are you going?"
Areli asked. But she already knew.

"You know where I'm going," Alex said. "I'm going to Nueva York!"
He flashed her a big grin and gave her a drawing of the two of them
in the yard with the chickens. "So you won't forget me," he said.

A few days later, he was gone.
Now, when she waited for
calls from Mamá and Papá, Areli
had to wait alone.

That fall, Areli started kindergarten at the
school near her abuela's house. She was so
proud to be at school! She learned to tie her
shoes and write the letters of the alphabet.
She played *al escondite* with her new friends.
She barely thought of Nueva York at all . . .

. . . until the day Abuela greeted her with tears in her eyes. "Areli, *mi'ja*. You're leaving us," she said. "Your mamá and papá are sending someone to take you to New York. To live with them at last." Abuela's voice was shaking.

ABARROTES

2 x 1

"I don't want to go to New York!" Areli said. "I want to stay here with you! And my friends. And my *home*. Please don't make me go, Abuela."

"If I could take care of you here, I would, my sweet. But I am old, and there is no future for you in Mexico. You don't understand now, but someday you will."

BIBLIOTECA

The next Saturday night's dinner was very sad.
Areli said goodbye to her cousins.

She said goodbye to her friends.

She said goodbye to the mountains and the chickens. "I'll never forget you," she said.

On Sunday morning, Abuela woke Areli at dawn. They held each other very tightly.

A man with kind eyes was waiting for Areli in the doorway. "This man is a friend of your mamá and papa's, and he will take you to America," Abuela said.

"Come, Areli," he said.

Areli stayed where she was. The man was a stranger to her.

"Be brave, Areli," Abuela said. Areli gave Abuela one more fierce hug. "I love you, *mi'ja*."

"I love you, Abuela!" said Areli.

Then she left for her new country.

CENTRAL DE
AUTOBUSES

Mamá cried very hard when she saw Areli. Areli ran to her, but Mamá didn't look like her picture at Abuela's house. Her hair was a different color, and it was curly. Papá had lines around his eyes. They held each other for a long time. Areli did not want to let go.

"Areli!" Alex said. "You made it! I can't wait to show you our house!" Alex was a lot taller, but he still had a smile that spread ear to ear.

Everything in New York was bigger and faster and noisier than in the mountains. It wasn't home at all.

Areli had to go to school, but the teachers did not know her name. She couldn't speak English, and when she tried, the words came out all wrong. She made friends with the other girls who could speak Spanish.

But she couldn't stop kids from teasing her.

"Areli's an illegal. They should take her back to Mexico."

"Areli can't read!"

"She's so backward!"

"Her mom cleans my house. She's our *maid*!"

Areli was ashamed. She had never felt this way before. *"No te preocupes, Areli,"* her friends said. *"No pueden hacerte daño."*

When she went home that night, Areli asked her mother what the kids meant when they said she was illegal.

"Illegal means against the law," her mother began.

"I'm not against the law!" Areli said.

"Of course you're not," said her mother. "But you were born in Mexico. So even though you are growing up here in America, you are not a citizen of this country."

"Do I get to be a citizen someday?" asked Areli.

"I hope so, *mi'ja*. I hope so."

Her mother wouldn't say anything else. So Areli asked Alex why she needed to be a citizen.

"If you're a citizen, you can do whatever Americans do," he said.

"What if I'm not?" Areli asked. She wasn't sure she wanted to hear the answer.

"Then I guess you could be taken back to Mexico," said Alex. He wouldn't look at her. "Without us."

Areli didn't understand. But she knew she should stay quiet about her first home in Mexico. She did not want to be sent back to Mexico all by herself. She did not want to break the law just by being who she was.

Areli had to work extra hard to learn her lessons in
a new language. It wasn't easy.

By second grade, she could count by fives.

In third grade, she learned about the Constitution.

By fourth grade, she could write a book report and read it aloud.

Pretty soon, it was hard for Areli to remember how the sun shone on the mountains at Abuela's house. Now she spoke English like any other girl from America. She played jump-rope games and watched TV shows.

She and Alex could get anywhere in the city on the subway. They rode the F train all the way to Coney Island, where she saw the ocean for the first time.

Every Fourth of July, she was mesmerized by the fireworks in the sky. She was a New Yorker.

In fifth grade, Areli's class went on a field trip.
They got on a boat and sailed into the Hudson River.
Areli's heart beat fast to see Ellis Island, where so
many immigrants had come before her.

On the tour of Ellis Island, Areli learned a lot. "More than twelve million immigrants passed through here on their way to America," said the tour guide. "Almost every one of us has family that came to this country from a foreign land."

On the boat ride back home, Areli thought about the tour guide's words. She pictured the millions of other people who had made the long journey to America, and how Lady Liberty welcomed them with her shining torch. She did not feel illegal. She felt like she was part of something very big.

On Saturday, she called her abuela in Mexico.

"Are you working hard?" Abuela asked.

"Very hard," Areli said. She told Abuela all about Ellis Island. "Those immigrants are part of America. Remember when you said I might have a brighter future here, Abuela? I think I understand now. And I think you were right."

That night, Areli looked out over the lights of New York City and dreamed of what she might do someday. She might be a writer and tell her story. She might be a teacher and help children who found themselves in this new land.

"I could do anything here," Areli said to the city sky. "Someday, I will."

GLOSSARY

abuela: grandmother

Día de los Muertos: Day of the Dead, a Mexican holiday celebrated on November 1–2, during which people gather to honor their loved ones who have passed. As part of the festivities, families and friends pray and build altars to assist the dead on their spiritual journeys.

el escondite: hide-and-seek

gracias: thank you

hola: hello

mi'ja: a contraction of the words "mi" ("my") and "hija" ("daughter"), colloquially used to address younger women affectionately

Navidad: Christmas

niña: girl

no pueden hacerte daño: they can't hurt you

no te preocupes: don't worry

pollo con frijoles: chicken with beans, which are a staple of Mexican cuisine

primas: female cousins

sí: yes

To immigrant families, especially my own, for the sacrifices they make to give us a shot at a better life —A.M.

Para Amelia, de tu familia que te quiere y piensa siempre en la distancia —L.U.

Text copyright © 2021 by Areli Morales
Jacket art and interior illustrations copyright © 2021 by Luisa Uribe

All rights reserved. Published in the United States by Random House Studio, an imprint of Random House Children's Books, a division of Penguin Random House LLC, New York. Random House Studio and the colophon are registered trademarks of Penguin Random House LLC.

Visit us on the Web! rhcbooks.com
Educators and librarians, for a variety of teaching tools, visit us at RHTeachersLibrarians.com

Library of Congress Cataloging-in-Publication Data is available upon request.
ISBN 978-1-9848-9399-4 (trade)
ISBN 978-1-9848-9400-7 (lib. bdg.)
ISBN 978-1-9848-9401-4 (ebook)

The artist used Adobe Photoshop to create the illustrations for this book.
The text of this book is set in 15-point Quasimoda.
Interior design by Rachael Cole

MANUFACTURED IN CHINA
10 9 8 7 6 5 4 3 2 1
First Edition